Table of Contents

Introduction 7

   About Slow Cookers 8

   Why Is Slow Cooker Food So Good? 9

   How to Clean Your Slow Cooker 11

Recipes 14

   Beef Dishes 15

      Shepherd's Winter Pie 16

      Homemade Beef Curry 18

      Healthy Beef Bolognese 19

      Mexican Chilli 20

      Hearty Beef Stew 22

      Goulash With Beef 24

      Tasty Stroganoff 25

   Lamb & Pork Dishes 26

      Fruity Braised Pork 27

      Tender Pork Ribs 29

      Stew With Sausage & Beans 30

      Lamb With Fragrant Rice 31

      Hearty, Warming Irish Stew 33

      Fizzy Cola Gammon 35

      Ginger Glazed Ham 37

      Easy Casserole With Sausage 38

      Tasty Leg Of Lamb 40

Exotic Lamb Curry..42

Tender Shoulder Of Pork...43

Poultry Dishes..44

Crispy Chicken & Tarragon Vegetables.......................................45

Potato & Chicken Stew..46

Asian Turkey Soup...47

Madeira Duck With Red Cabbage..49

South American Stew With Chicken..52

Tangy Pineapple & Duck Curry...53

Wine-Infused Turkey Fillets...54

Butter Chicken..57

Ultimate Chicken Tikka...59

Chicken With a Tasty Honey Twist..61

Chicken Soup Slow Cooker Style...62

No Hassle Espanyol Chicken..64

Easy Chicken Casserole...65

Tender Pulled Chicken..67

Continental Chicken Chasseur..68

Fragrant Thai Curry...70

Super-Fragrant Chicken Korma...71

Vegetarian Dishes..73

Vegetable Curry..74

Dhal With a Twist..75

Traditional Lentil & Carrot Soup...77

Mushroom & Garlic Spaghetti..78

Vegetable Tagine...79

Healthy Vegetable Stew..80

Tasty Veggie Lasagne...82

Slow Cooker Brunch Eggs...84

Slow Cooker Recipe Book UK 2021

Quick and Delicious Slow Cooker Recipes for the Whole Year incl. Desserts and Side Dishes

Amber C. Gardner

ISBN- 9798592353628

Seafood Dishes 85

    Corn Chowder With Haddock 86

    Spanish Paella Slow Cooker Style 87

    Tomato & Prawn Curry 89

Bonus – Desserts & Side Dishes 90

  Side Dishes 91

    Simple Slow Cooker Bread 92

    Tasty Aubergine Snacks 94

    Boozy Ginger Cabbage 96

    Cheesy Veggie Leaves 97

    Tasty Beans, No Baking Required! 98

  Desserts 99

    Easy & Healthy Yogurt 100

    Syrup Sponge 101

    Delicious Apple Crumble 103

    Effort Saving Rice Pudding 104

    Homemade Fudge 105

Conclusion 106

Disclaimer 108

Introduction

Have you recently found yourself craving something different? Are you tired of slaving over a hot stove when you return home from a busy day at work? Or, do you find it hard to stand in the kitchen and prepare a large meal for the family when you have a million other jobs to do at the same time?

You're not alone. Countless people face the same issues, but there is help at hand and it comes in the form of a slow cooker.

Slow cookers have been around for years, but they've recently enjoyed somewhat of a renaissance. Not only can you enjoy the supremely tender taste of meat and vegetables from a slow cooker, but you literally put everything inside, close the lid, and go about your business, sure in the knowledge that when you're ready to eat, your meal is there for the taking. What could be better?

When you search for the latest slow cookers on the market, you'll notice the huge range before you. This is good news, because it means you can find an appliance which suits your budget and the size of your family. You

can also choose a slow cooker with more functions, or less, depending upon what you want to achieve.

About Slow Cookers

Slow cookers are a kitchen device which allows you to cook your meals at low temperatures, over a longer period of time. Slow cookers run on the electric and use a simmering cooking technique. This means that your food is cooked for longer but in a gentler way, therefore tender and soft, rather than burnt or tough.

Slow cookers have several different settings, depending upon the model you opt for. They generally have two heat settings – low and high. You can choose whichever you want to go for, with low meaning that you cook for your food for around 7-8 hours, and high meaning that you can speed up the process and cook for around 4 hours. Each recipe will have different requirements, depending upon the ingredients you're using, but these are the general timings as a rule of thumb.

The low setting cooks your food at 87 degrees Celsius, and the high setting cooks at 148 degrees Celsius. As you can see, even the high setting doesn't reach extreme temperatures, which is why food is able to be left over a long period of time without any concerns about the state of it in the end.

Many people worry unnecessarily about the amount of electricity that a slow cooker uses. Despite the fact that slow cookers take hours to cook food, they're doing so at a slow rate and are therefore more energy efficient than a regular cooker. They use less electricity and allow your food to be far more delicious.

A slow cooker looks a lot like a large soup pot, with a lid on top and several electrical settings on the front. You'll find different makes and models, with different sizes available, depending upon how many people you're cooking for on a regular basis. A 3.5 litre slow cooker is the ideal size for two to three people within a household and is large enough to fit a regular sized chicken inside. However, if you have a large family, you might want to opt for a 6.5 litre slow cooker.

Why Is Slow Cooker Food So Good?

First things first, being able to prepare your food in the morning and then leave it all day long, knowing that when you return home you have a delicious meal waiting for you, is a major plus point in the busy society we live in. However, to understand why food cooked in a slow cooker is so delicious, you have to understand the method behind it all.

As we've mentioned, slow cookers cook your food at a lower temperature, over a longer period of time, using a simmering rather than a boiling. This method is ideal for meat which would otherwise turn out to be tough or

chewy, and turns it into a supremely tender, melt in your mouth cut. Even if you're not using meat, the flavours are easily released from the simplest of vegetables by using a slow cooker. The vitamins and minerals contained within foods are also retained, simply because you're not blasting the food at high temperatures.

So, slow cooker food is not only more tender and flavourful, but also healthier.

It's also worth mentioning that slow cookers and pressure cookers are two very different things. They often get confused because they look similar, but their cooking styles are distinct and they achieve completely different results. Pressure cookers use steam and its associated pressure to cook food very quickly, allowing you to have tender meat in a short amount of time. However, a slow cooker takes far longer and cooks at a slow simmer, therefore ensuring that the vitamins aren't lost, and neither is the taste.

If you find that a pressure cooker is a better option for you, you've never tried a slow cooker! The is a very good reason why slow cookers have become so famous and popular over recent years, despite the fact they've been around for a long time.

It's a fallacy to assume that you can only create stews and meat dishes in a slow cooker, as it's entirely possible to create a huge range of dishes, including lasagnes and desserts. Once you start perusing the range of recipes contained within the pages of this book, you'll see the huge

scope of possibility when you purchase a slow cooker. You can also start experimenting with your own recipes from scratch, because truly, the options are quite endless when it comes to the food you can create in a slow cooker.

How to Clean Your Slow Cooker

It's all very well and good knowing how to use your slow cooker and create delicious meals, but you also need to know how to clean it afterwards, ready for the next use. The good news is that cleaning your slow cooker is very easy and only takes a few minutes.

You can purchase specific slow cooker cleaning solutions, but you can also clean the appliance with a simple combination of water, white vinegar and baking soda. Check the instructions for your particular appliance before you begin, as some slow cookers have specific instructions that need to be followed, in order to avoid damaging the interior of the pot.

However, a general rule of thumb for cleaning a slow cooker very effectively is found below.

    ❧ Add water to the interior of your slow cooker, just above the maximum line for food

⮞ Take half a cup of white vinegar (or 1 cup if your slow cooker is a larger size) and pour inside

⮞ Add half a cup of baking soda (1 cup for a larger cooker)

⮞ Leave for a few minutes and then discard the mixture

⮞ Give your slow cooker a good scrub inside to remove any loosened pieces of grime or food

⮞ Rinse out with clean water and allow to dry

Be sure to store your slow cooker in a clean and dry part of your kitchen, to avoid any damp. By ensuring that you look after your slow cooker and follow any specific manufacturer instructions, it will last you far longer and allow you to create delicious meals time after time.

Some people choose to keep their slow cooker out on their countertop and that's fine, as long as you remember to give it a quick wipe down occasionally, if you don't use it for a few days. However, most models these days are pretty compact and that means they take up little space on workstations and in cupboards.

The rest of this book is going to be dedicated to showing you just what you can do with your new appliance. You'll find a range of delicious recipes to try for yourself, as well as a bonus section containing desserts and sides. Yes, you can make desserts! You'll be quite surprised at the scope of possibility and not only with your new slow cooker save you time, but it will enhance your cooking flavours too.

Now you know how to use your slow cooker and how to clean it, it's time to start whipping up a culinary storm, with less stress than you've ever cooked with before!

Recipes

Throughout the coming pages you'll find some truly delicious recipes to try in your slow cooker. From hearty curries to meat dishes, vegetarian options, and everything else in-between, you'll quickly see that slow cookers give you the ultimate taste, for very little effort.

Most recipes can be adjusted according to your own likes, e.g. if you prefer turkey rather than chicken, or lamb rather than beef, you can normally adjust the recipes to suit your tastes and preferences. However, do remember that this will change the nutritional information, if that is particularly important to you and your lifestyle.

BEEF DISHES

SHEPHERD'S WINTER PIE

SERVES 4
CALORIES: 438
FAT 10G
FIBRE 11G
PROTEIN 23G
CARBS 57G

INGREDIENTS

- 1 tbsp olive oil
- 250g beef mince
- 2 sliced carrots
- 1 chopped onion
- 3 sprigs of thyme
- 1 tbsp tomato paste
- 1 tsp Worcestershire sauce
- 1 tbsp flour
- 1 can of lentils
- 650g peeled potatoes, cut into medium sized chunks
- 2 tbsp crème fraiche
- 250g peeled sweet potatoes, cut into medium sized chunks

METHOD

1. Take a large frying pan and add the oil, over a medium heat
2. Add the thyme and onion and cook for 2 minutes
3. Add the carrots and cook until everything has softened
4. Add the mince and brown
5. Add the flour and cook for 2 more minutes
6. Add the tomato paste and combine
7. Add the lentils and combine
8. Add the Worcestershire sauce and combine everything well, before transferring to the slow cooker
9. Cook both the potatoes and the sweet potatoes in boiling water until soft
10. Drain and add the crème fraiche, creating a smooth mash
11. Add the potato in one layer over the top of the contents of the slow cooker
12. Cook for 5 hours on a low setting

HOMEMADE BEEF CURRY

SERVES 4
CALORIES: 425
FAT 30G
FIBRE 2G
PROTEIN 32G
CARBS 6G

INGREDIENTS

- 750g braising steak, cubed
- 3 tbsp olive oil
- 4 crushed garlic cloves
- 1 chopped onion
- 4 cardamom pods
- 1 stick of cinnamon
- 1 piece of grated ginger, around 5cm in size
- 1 tbsp coriander (ground)
- 2 tsp cumin
- 0.5 tsp turmeric (ground)
- 1 tsp chilli powder
- 1 can of coconut milk

METHOD

1. Take a large frying pan and add 2 tbsp of the olive oil, over a medium heat
2. Cook the beef until brown on all sides and then transfer to the slow cooker
3. Place the rest of the beef into the pan and cook the onion until soft
4. Add the ginger and garlic, combine and cook for another minute
5. Add the remaining spices, combine and cook for a further minute
6. Pour the coconut milk into the pan and combine everything well, allowing to simmer
7. Transfer the mixture into the slow cooker
8. Cook on high for 4 hours, or alternatively, cook for 8 hours on a low setting

HEALTHY BEEF BOLOGNESE

SERVES 12
CALORIES: 295
FAT 12G
FIBRE 4G
PROTEIN 34G
CARBS 13G

INGREDIENTS

- 4 tbsp olive oil
- 1.5kg minced beef
- 6 chopped rashers of bacon
- 3 chopped carrots
- 4 chopped onions
- 4 chopped sticks of celery
- 8 crushed cloves of garlic
- 500g sliced mushrooms

- 4 tbsp red wine vinegar
- 2 bay leaves
- 4 tbsp good quality red wine
- 4 cans of chopped tomatoes
- 2 tbsp mixed herbs (dried)
- 6 tbsp tomato paste
- 1 tbsp sugar

METHOD

1. Take a large frying pan and add the meats, cooking until brown
2. Transfer to your slow cooker
3. Place the garlic, onions, celery, carrots, tomato paste, mushrooms, herbs, tomatoes, wine, sugar, and red wine vinegar
4. Season and close the lid, cooking for 8 hours on a slow setting
5. Take the lid off and cook for another hour on a high setting

MEXICAN CHILLI

SERVES 4
CALORIES: 281
FAT 13G
FIBRE 6G
PROTEIN 19G
CARBS 18G

INGREDIENTS

- 500g good quality beef mince
- 1 chopped onion
- 3 tbsp olive oil
- 1 sliced red pepper
- 1 chopped celery stick
- 1 can of chopped tomatoes
- 400ml beef or vegetable stock
- 2 grated cloves of garlic
- 2 tsp cumin
- 2 tsp oregano (dried)
- 1 tsp paprika (smoked works best)
- 3 tbsp chipotle paste
- 2 cans of drained black beans
- 4 squares of good quality dark chocolate

METHOD

1. Take your slow cooker and set it to a low heat
2. Take a large frying pan and add half of the oil
3. Once hot, add the mince and cook until browned, transferring the meat to the slow cooker afterwards
4. Add the rest of the oil to the same pan and cook the pepper, celery and onion until soft
5. Add the paprika, cumin, garlic and combine, cooking for another minute
6. Add the mixture to the slow cooker
7. Add the chipotle paste, stock, chopped tomatoes, and oregano. Combine and season with a little salt and pepper to taste
8. Add the lid to the slow cooker and set to between 6-8 hours
9. During the last half an hour of cooking, add the chocolate and the beans, combining well

HEARTY BEEF STEW

SERVES 4
CALORIES: 474
FAT 25G
FIBRE 4G
PROTEIN 48G
CARBS 10G

INGREDIENTS

- 900g braising beef
- 600ml boiling water
- 1 chopped onion
- 2 whole bay leaves
- 2 tbsp olive oil
- 2 chopped celery sticks
- 3 cubed carrots
- 2 tbsp tomato paste
- 2 tbsp Worcestershire sauce
- Small bunch of chopped parsley
- 2 stock cubes (beef is preferable but vegetable is also acceptable)
- Pinch of thyme

METHOD

1. Add one tablespoon of olive oil to a frying pan and cook the celery and the onion until soft
2. Add the bay leaves, thyme, and the carrots and cook for another two minutes
3. Add the Worcestershire sauce and tomato paste and stir
4. Add the boiling water and combine everything well
5. Remove the pan from the heat and transfer the contents to the slow cooker
6. Crumble the stock cubes over the pan and stir
7. Take another frying pan and cook the beef in the remaining tablespoon of oil until brown
8. Transfer the beef to the slow cooker
9. Set the slow cooker to low and cook for 10 hours. Alternatively, set to high and cook for just 4 hours

GOULASH WITH BEEF

SERVES 8
CALORIES: 581
FAT 32G
FIBRE 6G
PROTEIN 54G
CARBS 17G

INGREDIENTS

- 2kg cubes of stewing steak
- 3 tbsp olive oil
- 2 chopped onions
- 3 crushed garlic cloves
- 4 chopped peppers (mixed)
- 2 tsp caraway seeds

- 2 tsp smoked paprika
- 2 tbsp plain flour
- 5 tbsp tomato paste
- 500ml stock, beef or vegetable
- 4 chopped tomatoes
- 300ml sour cream

METHOD

1. Take the slow cooker and set to a low heat
2. Take a large frying pan and add 2 tablespoons of the oil on medium heat
3. Cook the beef on all sides to sear before setting aside
4. Add the rest of the oil and cook the onions until brown
5. Add the garlic and peppers and cook for another 10 minutes
6. Add the spices and the flour and stir well, cooking for another 2 minutes
7. Add the tomato paste, the stock and the tomatoes, stirring once more
8. Allow the mixture to reach a simmer and then transfer to the slow cooker
9. Add the beef and cover
10. Cook for 7 hours
11. Add the sour cream just before serving and stir gently

TASTY STROGANOFF

SERVES 4
CALORIES: 988
FAT 61G
FIBRE 7G
PROTEIN 31G
CARBS 76G

INGREDIENTS

- 2 tbsp olive oil
- 750g stewing steak, cut into thin strips
- 2 crushed garlic cloves
- 2 sliced onions
- 1 tbsp mustard
- 50g unsalted butter
- 1 stock cube, beef or vegetable
- 2 tsp cornflour
- 200g halved chestnut mushrooms
- 200g sour cream

METHOD

1. Take the slow cooker and set to low
2. Take a large frying pan and add the beef, cooking to brown
3. Once browned, place the meat into the slow cooker
4. Place the garlic and onion into the frying pan and cook until soft
5. Transfer into the slow cooker
6. Add the mustard and stock, combining everything well
7. Pour water into the slow cooker, so that you just cover the contents
8. Place the lid on and cook for 8 hours on low. Alternatively, you can cook for 6 hours on high

LAMB & PORK DISHES

FRUITY BRAISED PORK

SERVES 8
CALORIES: 530
FAT 36G
FIBRE 1G
PROTEIN 40G
CARBS 11G

INGREDIENTS

- 2 tbsp olive oil
- Pork shoulder, about 1.5kg in weight and cut into large pieces
- 5 tbsp soy sauce
- 5 tbsp rice wine
- 2 tbsp tomato paste
- 1 piece of root ginger, around 5cm in size
- 1 chopped red chilli
- 5 cloves of garlic
- 2 star anise
- 1.5 tsp five spice
- 500ml chicken stock
- 2 tbsp sugar
- A few sliced spring onions
- 1 stick of cinnamon
- 6 stoned and halved plums, make sure they're ripe

METHOD

1. Take a large bowl and add the soy sauce, half the chilli, half the garlic, and half the ginger, as well as the rice wine, combining well

2. Add the pork pieces and coat generously and marinade for a few hours at least, or up to 24 hours

3. Take a large frying pan and add the oil, spring onions, chilli, cinnamon, garlic, ginger, five spice, star anise and the sugar, combining well

4. Add the tomato paste and combine, cooking until everything is soft

5. Add the pork to the pan and seal on all sides

6. Transfer everything to the slow cooker, along with the rest of the marinade and the stock

7. Cover the slow cooker and set to low, cooking for 9 hours

8. Halfway through cooking, skim away any fat you can see

9. After 8 hours have passed, add the plums to the slow cooker and give everything a stir

10. Once cooked, remove the meat and plums and set aside

11. Turn the slow cooker up to high and cook for another 15 minutes, allowing the sauce to thicken

12. Place the meat and plums back inside the pan and stir

TENDER PORK RIBS

SERVES 4
CALORIES: 414
FAT 24G
FIBRE 1.4G
PROTEIN 23G
CARBS 24G

INGREDIENTS

- 350g BBQ sauce
- 2 bay leaves
- 2 stock cubes, the pork variety work very well
- 1.5kg pork ribs
- 1 tsp mustard seeds
- 1 tsp peppercorns
- 1 tsp coriander seeds
- 1.5 litres of water

METHOD

1. Add all ingredients to your slow cooker, except for the BBQ sauce
2. Add just 4 tbsp of the BBQ sauce and combine everything well
3. Add the water and combine once more
4. Set your slow cooker to low and cook for 9 hours
5. Set your regular oven to 220C
6. Take a baking tray and cover with foil
7. Take the ribs out of the slow cooker and place on the tray
8. Coat with the rest of the BBQ sauce, taking care not to allow the meat to fall away from the bone too much
9. Place in the oven for 20 minutes, until crispy

STEW WITH SAUSAGE & BEANS

SERVES 4
CALORIES: 355
FAT 15G
FIBRE 10G
PROTEIN 20G
CARBS 37G

INGREDIENTS

- 2 cans of mixed beans
- 2 cans of chopped tomatoes
- 8 chipolata sausages

- 1 tbsp sugar
- 2 tsp oregano
- 1 tsp basil

METHOD

1. Take a frying pan and cook your sausages for a few minutes on both sides, until brown
2. Transfer the sausages to the slow cooker
3. Add the rest of the ingredients and combine well
4. Set your slow cooker to low and cook for 8 hours

LAMB WITH FRAGRANT RICE

SERVES 4
CALORIES: 584
FAT 24G
FIBRE 3G
PROTEIN 32G
CARBS 65G

INGREDIENTS

- 1 tbsp olive oil
- 500g lamb, cut into cubes
- 250g rice, basmati works best for this recipe
- 1 sliced onion
- 1 stock cube, vegetable or lamb
- 2 broken cinnamon sticks
- A few chopped mint leaves
- 12 dried apricots
- A few pine nuts
- 500ml boiling water

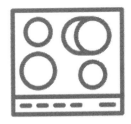

METHOD

1. Take a large frying pan and add the pine nuts, dry frying them for a few minutes on each side
2. Place to one side
3. Add the oil to the pan and cook the spices, cinnamon and the onion for around 10 minutes
4. Add the lamb and turn up the heat a little, browning on all sides
5. Transfer everything you've cooked to the slow cooker
6. Add the rice and combine everything well
7. Add the boiling water and the stock cube, stirring well
8. Add the apricots and add a little salt and pepper to season
9. Turn your slow cooker to low and cook for 4 hours
10. Serve with the pine nuts and mint leaves

HEARTY, WARMING IRISH STEW

SERVES 6
CALORIES: 673
FAT 39G
FIBRE 7G
PROTEIN 40G
CARBS 40G

INGREDIENTS

- 1 tbsp olive oil
- 900g stewing lamb, cut into chunks
- 200g streaky bacon (smoked works well) cut into regular sized pieces
- 5 chopped carrots
- 3 sliced onions
- 3 bay leaves
- 1 chopped leek
- 6 chopped potatoes
- 700ml stock, lamb works best
- Bunch of fresh thyme
- Knob of unsalted butter
- 85g pearl barley

METHOD

1. Take a large frying pan and add the oil
2. Cook the bacon on both sides and add to the slow cooker
3. Add the lamb to the frying pan and brown all over, before adding to the slow cooker
4. Add the carrots, potatoes, thyme, onions, bay leaves, and stock to the slow cooker
5. Add enough water to cover over the meat and combine
6. Place the lid on the cooker and set to low for 7 hours
7. Add the leek and the pearl barley, combining
8. Cook for an hour on a high setting
9. Add the butter and stir just before serving

FIZZY COLA GAMMON

SERVES 8
CALORIES: 329
FAT 15G
FIBRE 1G
PROTEIN 33G
CARBS 16G

INGREDIENTS

- 1.5kg gammon joint, without bones
- 1 chopped carrot
- 1 chopped onion
- 1 chopped stick of celery
- 2 litres of full fat cola
- 1 stick of cinnamon
- 1 bay leaf
- 0.5 tbsp peppercorns
- 2 tbsp mustard, wholegrain works best
- 150ml maple syrup
- 2 tbsp red wine vinegar

METHOD

1. Turn your slow cooker to a low setting
2. Add the meat into your slow cooker and pour the cola over the top
3. Add the onion, celery, carrot, peppercorns, bay leaf, and the cinnamon stick and combine
4. Cover and cook on low for 5.5 hours
5. Discard of the liquid and allow the meat to cool down
6. Now heat your regular oven to 190 C
7. Place the meat into a roasting tin and score the top
8. Take a mixing jug and combine the mustard, maple syrup and vinegar
9. Pour half of the mixture over the top of the meat and cook for 15 minutes
10. Pour the rest of the mixture over the meat and cook for another half an hour
11. Allow the meat to rest for 10 minutes before serving

GINGER GLAZED HAM

SERVES 8
CALORIES: 363
FAT 14G
FIBRE 1G
PROTEIN 27G
CARBS 31G

INGREDIENTS

- 1.5kg joint of gammon
- 1 sliced onion
- 1 tbsp mustard
- 3 tbsp ginger preserve
- 10 whole cloves
- 1.5 litres of ginger beer

METHOD

1. Arrange the cloves and the onion in the slow cooker and add the meat on top
2. Add the ginger beer into the slow cooker
3. Cook for 7 hours on a low setting
4. Heat your regular oven to 200 C
5. Take the skin off the meat to show the fat
6. Score and stud with extra cloves
7. Take a small mixing bowl and add the ginger and mustard to create a paste
8. Brush over the meat
9. Cook for 20 minutes

EASY CASSEROLE WITH SAUSAGE

SERVES 4
CALORIES: 449
FAT 28G
FIBRE 8G
PROTEIN 17G
CARBS 27G

INGREDIENTS

- 2 tbsp olive oil
- 12 halved chipolata sausages
- 2 chopped red onions
- 1 chopped stick of celery
- 1 peeled sweet potato, cubed
- 4 sliced carrots
- 1 tbsp tomato paste
- 1 can of tomatoes
- 250ml boiling water
- 1 stock cube, beef or vegetable
- 1 sprig of thyme
- 1 sprig of rosemary

METHOD

1. Take a medium frying pan and add the oil, over a low heat
2. Add the onion and celery and soften
3. Once soft, add to the slow cooker
4. Cook the carrots in the frying pan until a little soft and place in the slow cooker also
5. Add the sausages to the frying pan and brown on all sides, before transferring to the slow cooker
6. Add the can of tomatoes and the sweet potato to the slow cooker, combining everything well
7. Add the tomato paste to the frying pan and add the boiling water, giving everything a stir
8. Pour everything into the slow cooker, along with the stock cube, the herbs and a little seasoning
9. Cook on a low setting for 8 hours, or alternatively, a high setting for 4 hours

TASTY LEG OF LAMB

SERVES 6
CALORIES: 574
FAT 37G
FIBRE 1G
PROTEIN 43G
CARBS 9G

INGREDIENTS

- 2 tbsp olive oil
- 30g butter
- 300ml stock (lamb)
- 1 leg of lamb, boneless. Around 1.3kg in weight
- 200ml good quality red wine
- 2 sliced red onions
- 2 sliced cloves of garlic
- 5 rosemary sprigs
- 5 thyme sprigs

METHOD

1. Take a large frying pan and add the oil, over a medium heat
2. Transfer the lamb to the pan and cook on each side for 5 minutes, until browned
3. Take your slow cooker and set it to a low temperature
4. Take a medium saucepan and add the butter, allowing it to melt
5. Add the flour and mix well
6. Use a whisk to combine the stock into the mixture, before adding the wine and allowing the mixture to reach boiling point
7. Add the thyme, rosemary, garlic and onion into the slower cooker
8. Place the lamb inside
9. Slowly pour the stock mixture over the top
10. Close the cooker and cook for 8 hours
11. Once cooked, carefully take the lamb out of the slow cooker and shred or slice, serving with the juices

EXOTIC LAMB CURRY

SERVES 2
CALORIES: 568
FAT 19G
FIBRE 13G
PROTEIN 43G
CARBS 49G

INGREDIENTS

- 2 cubed lamb fillets
- 3 tbsp curry paste (Madras works best)
- 1 sliced onion
- 25g lentils (red)
- 1 can of chopped tomatoes
- 1 can of chickpeas
- 2 tsp bouillon powder (vegetable)
- 75g kale
- 1 tbsp fresh grated ginger
- 1 tsp cumin seeds
- 1 stick of cinnamon
- 1 large cup of water

METHOD

1. Transfer all ingredients into your slow cooker and combine well
2. Add a large cup of water and stir once more
3. Cover the slow cooker and place into the refrigerator for a few hours, or overnight if possible
4. Once you're ready to cook, give everything another good stir and then set on low, cooking for 6 hours

TENDER SHOULDER OF PORK

SERVES 8
CALORIES: 245
FAT 9G
FIBRE 0.3G
PROTEIN 34G
CARBS 1G

INGREDIENTS

- Pork shoulder, around 1.5kg in weight
- 2 tbsp olive oil
- 250ml stock, chicken or vegetable
- 250ml good quality white wine
- 2 rosemary sprigs
- 4 bay leaves
- 1 whole bulb of garlic (peeled)
- 1 tsp peppercorns

METHOD

1. Take a large frying pan and cook the pork over a medium heat until brown on all sides, seasoning as you go
2. Transfer the pork to the slow cooker
3. Transfer the rest of the ingredients into the slow cooker and combine well
4. Cook on a low setting for 8 hours
5. Once cooked, remove the pork and use two forks to shred apart
6. Transfer the meat back into the slow cooker to stir back into the sauces

POULTRY DISHES

CRISPY CHICKEN & TARRAGON VEGETABLES

SERVES 2
CALORIES: 386
FAT 16G
FIBRE 3G
PROTEIN 38G
CARBS 23G

INGREDIENTS

- 1 tbsp olive oil
- 2 chicken fillets
- 500ml chicken stock
- 200g sliced new potatoes
- 2 tbsp crème fraiche
- 200g pack of mixed vegetables
- A few chopped tarragon leaves

METHOD

1. Take a large frying pan and add the oil
2. Brown the chicken on all sides, for around 5 minutes on each side
3. Add the potatoes to the pan and combine into the juices
4. Remove the potatoes from the pan and arrange along the base of the slow cooker
5. Place the chicken on top of the potatoes
6. Add the stock and cover the slow cooker
7. Set to high and cook for 1.5 hours
8. Take the chicken out of the pan and add the vegetables, combining well
9. Add the chicken back inside and cover the slow cooker
10. Cook for another hour
11. Add the creme fraiche, a little salt and pepper and the tarragon

POTATO & CHICKEN STEW

SERVES 6
CALORIES: 284
FAT 13G
FIBRE 2G
PROTEIN 2G
CARBS 12G

INGREDIENTS

- 12 chopped rashers of streaky bacon
- 6 chicken thighs, bones left in
- 1 tbsp olive oil
- 250g halved new potatoes
- 200g shallots
- 500ml chicken stock
- 200ml good quality white wine
- A handful of sprigs of thyme
- The juice of a lemon
- 2 tbsp chopped tarragon

METHOD

1. Take a large pan and add the oil over a medium heat
2. Cook the chicken thighs for 10 minutes on all sides, until browned
3. Add the bacon and shallots and allow those to brown too
4. Transfer to your slow cooker, along with the lemon juice and half of the tarragon
5. Set to high and cook for 6 hours
6. Add the rest of the tarragon and season with salt and pepper

ASIAN TURKEY SOUP

SERVES 4
CALORIES: 334
FAT 6G
FIBRE 4G
PROTEIN 33G
CARBS 36G

INGREDIENTS

- The carcass of 1 turkey, with zero meat (you can use chicken if you prefer)
- 50g sliced ginger
- 3 star anise
- 2 halved onions
- 0.5 tbsp coriander seeds
- 2 sticks of cinnamon
- 2 whole cloves
- 2 tbsp sugar
- 3 tbsp fish sauce
- 200g rice noodles, the flat variety work well
- 400g sliced and cooked turkey
- 2 sliced red chillies
- 100g blanched beansprouts
- A few chopped mint leaves
- A few chopped coriander leaves
- A few chopped basil leaves

- 1 sliced lime
- 4 litres of boiling water

METHOD

1. Take a large frying pan and add the onion and ginger
2. Cook over a high heat, dry
3. Once the onion and ginger are soft, transfer to the slow cooker
4. Set the slow cooker to low
5. Place all spices into the frying pan and cook for a few minutes, before transferring to the slow cooker
6. Place the turkey or chicken carcass into the slow cooker and add the boiling water, making sure that the carcass is covered
7. Place the lid on the slow cooker and cook for 10 hours
8. Remove the stock from the slow cooker and run it through a strainer
9. Keep the stock and discard the rest
10. Add the sugar and fish sauce to the stock and combine well
11. Cook your noodles according to instructions on the pattern and place into your serving bowls
12. Add the beansprouts and pour the stock into each bowl
13. Distribute the chilli, lime slices, and the herbs between the bowls

MADEIRA DUCK WITH RED CABBAGE

SERVES 2
CALORIES: 890
FAT 64G
FIBRE 6G
PROTEIN 48G
CARBS 27G

INGREDIENTS

- 2 large duck legs
- 1 can of goose fat
- 2 tsp black peppercorns
- 25g salt
- 4 bay leaves
- Half pint of groundnut oil
- 1 tsp thyme
- Knob of butter
- 300g chicken stock
- 1 tsp flour
- 2 tsp madeira
- 400g shredded red cabbage
- 2 tbsp red wine vinegar
- 5 chopped juniper berries
- 4 halved shallots
- 25g raisins
- 1 tbsp redcurrant jelly
- Juice of 1 orange

METHOD

1. Prepare the duck herb rub around 24 hours before you intend to eat it
2. Take a mixing bowl and add the salt and peppercorns and combine well
3. Coat the duck legs in the mixture and cover, leaving overnight in the refrigerator
4. Remove the salt from the duck legs before cooking
5. Add them to your slow cooker along with the thyme, bay leaves and the goose fat (reserving 2 tablespoons for the cabbage)
6. Place the lid on top and cook on a low setting for 12 hours
7. Meanwhile, take a small pan and add the butter over a medium heat
8. Add the 2 chopped shallots and cook for around 8 minutes, stirring occasionally
9. Add the flour and keep stirring until it turns a little brown
10. Add the stock and whisk until thick
11. Add the madeira and cook for another 2 minutes
12. Sieve the mixture and place to one side
13. Take another saucepan and add the 2 tablespoons of goose fat you kept to one side
14. Add the 4 halved shallots and combine
15. Add the juniper berries and combine, then add the cabbage and stir well
16. Turn the heat up a little higher and allow the cabbage to wilt and soften
17. Add the orange juice, raisins, redcurrant jelly and the vinegar and combine
18. Cover the pan and cook for quarter of an hour, stirring occasionally
19. Remove the duck legs and strain away the fat
20. Preheat your regular oven to 200C

21. Take a roasting tin with a wire rack on top and place the duck on top of the rack

22. Place the thyme on top of the duck

23. Place in the oven for 30 minutes, until the skin has turned a little crispy and golden

24. To serve, add the cabbage to the plate and place the duck on top of it

25. Ladle the gravy on top and enjoy!

METHOD

1. Take a large frying pan and heat the oil over a medium heat
2. Add the garlic and onions and cook for 5 minutes, stirring occasionally
3. Add the courgettes, peppers, tomatoes, tomato paste, basil and bouillon and combine well, cooking for another 5 minutes
4. Lay the slices of aubergine on the bottom of the slow cooker
5. Add the pasta sheets on top
6. Add some of the cooked mixture on top of the pasta sheets
7. Continue to build your lasagne alternating between aubergine, pasta, and the cooked mixture
8. Place the lid on the slow cooker and cook for 3 hours on high
9. Once cooked, sprinkle the cheese over the top and place the lid back on for a few minutes, to melt the cheese
10. Serve with a sprinkling of basil

SLOW COOKER BRUNCH EGGS

SERVES 4
CALORIES: 165
FAT 8G
FIBRE 3G
PROTEIN 9G
CARBS 13G

INGREDIENTS

- 1 tbsp olive oil
- 1 sliced red pepper
- 1 sliced red chili pepper
- 4 whole eggs
- 2 sliced onions
- 8 small tomatoes, cherry tomatoes are best
- 2 tbsp milk, skimmed works well
- 1 slice of crusty bread cut into cubes

METHOD

1. Coat the inside of the slow cooker with a little oil
2. Add the rest of the oil to large frying pan and heat on a medium heat
3. Add the red pepper, chilli pepper and onions and cook until soft
4. Transfer into the slow cooker, along with the tomatoes and bread, combining well
5. Crack the eggs into a small dish and whisk, adding the milk until smooth
6. Pour the egg mixture over the slow cooker contents and combine
7. Place the lid on the slow cooker and cook on low for 5 hours

SEAFOOD DISHES

CORN CHOWDER WITH HADDOCK

SERVES 4
CALORIES: 334
FAT 6G
FIBRE 4G
PROTEIN 33G
CARBS 36G

INGREDIENTS

- 2 fillets of smoked haddock
- 2 chopped rashers of bacon
- 1 chopped onion
- 2 medium chopped potatoes
- 140g frozen corn
- A small knob of butter
- 500ml semi-skimmed milk

METHOD

1. Take a frying pan and add the butter of a medium heat, until melted
2. Add the potatoes, onions, and bacon, and cook for 5 minutes
3. Transfer to the slow cooker along with the milk, combining well
4. Set your slow cooker to high and cook for 3 hours
5. Add the corn and stir carefully
6. Place the fish fillets on top of the mixture and cover the slow cooker
7. Cook for another half an hour

SPANISH PAELLA SLOW COOKER STYLE

SERVES 6
CALORIES: 517
FAT 21G
FIBRE 5G
PROTEIN 31G
CARBS 46G

INGREDIENTS

- 4 chicken thighs, without bones and cut into slices
- 2 tbsp olive oil
- 240g sliced chorizo
- 2 crushed garlic cloves
- 1 sliced onion
- 150ml good quality white wine
- 1 tbsp smoked paprika (the sweet version works well)
- 1 can of chopped tomatoes
- 400ml chicken stock
- 300g paella rice
- 200g frozen king prawns (you can use fresh if you prefer)
- 150g peas (frozen)
- A handful of chopped parsley leaves

METHOD

1. Select the low setting on your slow cooker
2. Take the frying pan and add the oil, cooking over a medium heat
3. Add the chorizo and the chicken and cook for 10 minutes
4. Transfer the mixture to the slow cooker
5. Cook the onion in the pan until soft
6. Add the paprika and garlic and combine, cooking for 2 minutes
7. Add the wine into the pan and allow to reduce to around half the amount on a simmer
8. Transfer to the slow cooker and add the tomatoes, stock and the rice
9. Cover over and cook for 1.5 hours
10. Add the prawns and the peas and allow to cook for another half an hour
11. If the rice needs more time, you can cook for another half an hour
12. Serve with chopped parsley

TOMATO & PRAWN CURRY

SERVES 4
CALORIES: 236
FAT 0G
FIBRE 6G
PROTEIN 24G
CARBS 18G

INGREDIENTS

- 1 tbsp olive oil
- 400g king prawns, raw and shelled
- 2 onions, cut into large wedges
- 6 tomatoes, cut into large wedges
- 6 chopped cloves of garlic

- 1 piece of chopped root ginger, about 5cm
- 250g peas, frozen work well
- A few chopped coriander leaves
- 3 tbsp curry paste

METHOD

1. Take your food processor and add the olive oil, garlic, ginger, and curry paste, along with most of the wedges of tomato (leave around 8 to one side)
2. Place the paste into your slow cooker and combine with the onions
3. Cover the slow cooker and set to high, cooking for 3 hours
4. Add the rest of the tomato wedges, the peas and the uncooked prawns, and combine
5. Cover again and cook for another 1 hour, making sure that the prawns are well cooked
6. Serve with the coriander leaves on top

Bonus – Desserts & Side Dishes

SIDE DISHES

SIMPLE SLOW COOKER BREAD

SERVES 4
CALORIES: 179
FAT 1G
FIBRE 5G
PROTEIN 8G
CARBS 32G

INGREDIENTS

- 1 sachet of dried yeast (7g is enough)
- 500g wholemeal flour, or you can also use strong white flour
- 1g salt
- 350ml lukewarm water

METHOD

1. Take a large mixing bowl and add the flour, salt, and yeast
2. Create a small hole in the middle of the mixture and add the majority of the water
3. Slowly combine the mixture with your hands until a sticky yet easy to work dough is achieved
4. If needed, add slightly more water
5. Turn the dough out onto a floured work surface and knead for up to 10 minutes. The dough should be non-sticky and elastic
6. Create a ball with the dough and place it on a baking tray covered with baking paper
7. Carefully place the bread inside the slow cooker
8. Place the lid on the slow cooker and set to high
9. Cook for 2 hours
10. Remove the bread using the edges of the baking paper to help you
11. Your bread should be crusty, but not overly so

TASTY AUBERGINE SNACKS

SERVES 6
CALORIES: 269
FAT 20G
FIBRE 6G
PROTEIN 8G
CARBS 11G

INGREDIENTS

- 500g fresh aubergines, cut into slices
- 4 tbsp olive oil, plus extra 2 tbsp for the dressing
- 2 crushed garlic cloves
- 1 sliced red onion
- 1 sliced fennel bulb
- 1 tsp coriander seeds
- 300g tomatoes, cut into quarters
- 50g sundried tomatoes
- Bunch of chopped, fresh parsley
- Bunch of chopped, fresh chives
- 2 tsp capers
- Juice of 1 lemon

METHOD

1. Place 2 tablespoons of olive oil into the slow cooker
2. Arrange the red onions and the garlic inside the base of the cooker
3. Brush the sliced aubergines with olive oil and arrange them on top of the other slow cooker ingredients already inside
4. Add the onions, slices of fennel and the sundried tomatoes into the slow cooker
5. Add the coriander seeds and a little salt and pepper
6. Set your slow cooker to low and cook for 8 hours
7. Add the parsley, chives, lemon juice and capers into a food processer and blitz to create a dressing
8. Remove the aubergine mixture and arrange on a plate
9. Drizzle the dressing over the top

BOOZY GINGER CABBAGE

SERVES 6
CALORIES: 165
FAT 8G
FIBRE 6G
PROTEIN 3G
CARBS 18G

INGREDIENTS

- 1kg sized, sliced red cabbage
- 2 sliced apples
- 1 sliced red onion
- 1 piece of fresh, grated ginger, about 5cm in size
- 100ml stock, either vegetable or chicken
- 50g butter
- 0.5 tbsp brown sugar
- 2 tsp crushed coriander seeds
- 1 star anise
- 1 can of ginger beer (the alcoholic variety)
- 2 tbsp apple cider vinegar

METHOD

1. Set your slow cooker to low
2. Place all ingredients inside the cooker and season with a little salt and pepper
3. Combine everything
4. Cook for 5 hours
5. Take the lid off the slow cooker and set to a high temperature
6. Cook for an extra hour before serving

CHEESY VEGGIE LEAVES

SERVES 8
CALORIES: 370
FAT 34G
FIBRE 4G
PROTEIN 6G
CARBS 7G

INGREDIENTS

- 400g kale
- 0.5 tbsp olive oil
- 50g butter
- 3 sliced leeks
- 1 sliced onion
- 400ml double cream
- 100ml vegetable stock
- 1 tsp Dijon mustard
- 40g grated hard cheese
- A pinch of nutmeg

METHOD

1. Set your slow cooker to low
2. Take a frying pan and add the oil and butter
3. Once melted, add the onion and cook until soft
4. Add the kale and cook for another 5 minutes
5. Transfer the contents of the pan to the slow cooker
6. Add most of the cream and vegetable stock, combining well
7. Place the lid on the slow cooker and cook for 3 hours, giving it a stir every so often
8. Add the rest of the cream, the cheese, mustard and the nutmeg and stir before serving

TASTY BEANS, NO BAKING REQUIRED!

SERVES 2
CALORIES: 399
FAT 11G
FIBRE 0G
PROTEIN 19G
CARBS 60G

INGREDIENTS

- 1 tsp olive oil
- 1 can of cannellini beans
- 1 sliced onion
- 1 tbsp brown sugar
- 2 rashers of chopped bacon
- 200ml vegetable stock

METHOD

1. Take a frying pan and add the oil, heating over a medium heat
2. Cook the bacon and onion until the onion is soft and the bacon is cooked
3. Add the tomatoes, stock and sugar and combine everything well
4. Transfer the mixture to your slow cooker and add the beans
5. Combine well and place the lid on the slow cooker
6. Set to low and cook for 10 hours

DESSERTS

EASY & HEALTHY YOGURT

SERVES 2 LITRES
CALORIES: 120
FAT 5G
FIBRE 0G
PROTEIN 8G
CARBS 11G

INGREDIENTS

- 100ml yogurt – it must be the live variety
- 2 litres of milk – make sure you choose the full fat, whole version

METHOD

1. Add the milk to the slow cooker
2. Place the lid on the slow cooker and set to high
3. Cook for around 2 hours, until the milk reaches 82 degrees C
4. Turn the heat off and allow the milk to cool down for around 2 to 3 hours
5. Remove one cup of the milk and combine with the live yogurt
6. Return the mixture to the slow cooker and combine well
7. Place the lid back on the slow cooker and wrap in a large towel
8. Set the cooker aside for up to 12 hours to allow the yogurt to set

SYRUP SPONGE

SERVES 4
CALORIES: 763
FAT 43G
FIBRE 1G
PROTEIN 10G
CARBS 90G

INGREDIENTS

- 3 tbsp golden syrup
- 175g soft, unsalted butter
- 175g sugar
- 3 beaten eggs
- 2 tbsp milk
- 175g self-raising flour
- 1 tbsp white breadcrumbs
- Zest of 1 lemon

METHOD

1. Take a pudding dish and grease well
2. Take a small bowl and add the breadcrumbs and golden syrup, combining well
3. Take another bowl and add the butter, softening until easily workable
4. Add the lemon zest and gradually add the eggs
5. Add the flour and fold in gently
6. Add the milk and combine once more
7. Transfer the mixture to your pudding dish
8. Cover the top with greased foil and make a tent effect in the middle to allow rising
9. Tie string around the top to hold the foil in place
10. Place your pudding dish into the slow cooker
11. Add boiling water around the sides, reaching around halfway
12. Set the slow cooker to high and cook for 4 hours

DELICIOUS APPLE CRUMBLE

SERVES 6
CALORIES: 447
FAT 16G
FIBRE 6G
PROTEIN 6G
CARBS 75G

INGREDIENTS

- 1kg of peeled, cored, and sliced apples
- The juice of 1 orange
- 4 tbsp apricot jam
- 100g flour (plain)

- 140g porridge oats
- 100g unsalted butter
- 100g brown sugar
- 1 tbsp golden syrup
- 1 tsp cinnamon

METHOD

1. Place the jam, orange juice and apples into your slow cooker
2. Set the slow cooker to low and cook for 4 hours
3. Meanwhile, take a large mixing bowl and add the cinnamon, oats, and flour
4. Rub the butter into the mixture to create a crumble
5. Add the sugars and rub everything together once more
6. Once the apples are cooked, transfer into a regular baking dish in an even layer
7. Add the crumble mixture over the top evenly
8. Place the dish under the grill for a few minutes, until the crumble turns golden brown

EFFORT SAVING RICE PUDDING

SERVES 4
CALORIES: 399
FAT 11G
FIBRE 0G
PROTEIN 19G
CARBS 60G

INGREDIENTS

- 25g sugar
- 25g butter

- 1.2 litres of whole milk
- 110g pudding rice

METHOD

1. Grease the inside of your slow cooker with some of the butter
2. Place all ingredients inside and combine well
3. Place the lid on and set to high for 4 hours, stirring at the halfway point to unstick any pieces of rice

HOMEMADE FUDGE

MAKE 35 PIECES
CALORIES: 120
FAT 6G
FIBRE 1G
PROTEIN 2G
CARBS 14G

INGREDIENTS

- 250g chopped dark chocolate
- 250g chopped milk chocolate
- 1 tsp vanilla extract
- 100g brown sugar
- 1 can of condensed milk (375g)

METHOD

1. Set your slow cooker to low
2. Add the milk and dark chocolate, sugar, vanilla and the milk to the cooker and stir well
3. Add a pinch of salt and combine once more
4. Cover the slow cooker and cook for 1 hour, giving it a stir every 20 minutes
5. Meanwhile, grease a square baking tin and line with baking paper
6. Transfer the fudge to the tin and place in the refrigerator for 4 hours
7. Once set, cut into 35 equal pieces

Conclusion

And there we have it, a range of delicious recipes you can recreate in your own slow cooker. Take your time exploring and choose your favourite recipes to begin with, before branching out to some more in-depth choices as you go along.

The beauty of using a slow cooker is that you get that truly delicious fusion of flavours that cooking in a regular oven or on a hob simply doesn't give you. The slow simmering allows the spices and the meat to tenderise and infuse, and when the cooking time is up, you have meat that is so soft, it melts in your mouth, along with vegetables that are so bursting with flavour, you'll wonder why you never invested in this appliance before!

When shopping for a slow cooker, remember to do your research. Choose an appliance which is large enough for your family, but not so large that your food is going to be lost inside it! The good news is that even the largest capacity slow cookers are pretty compact these days, so there's no issue with storage or the machine dominating your workspace in a negative way.

Most recipes work well in a slow cooker, and if you find that some of the ingredients in the recipes above aren't your favourites, experiment with taking some away and adding different ones in. This is your slow cooker, and your gastronomical experiment alone!

Have fun with your slow cooker and remember to make the very most of that special way of cooking.

Disclaimer

This book contains opinions and ideas of the author and is meant to teach the reader informative and helpful knowledge while due care should be taken by the user in the application of the information provided. The instructions and strategies are possibly not right for every reader and there is no guarantee that they work for everyone. Using this book and implementing the information/recipes therein contained is explicitly your own responsibility and risk. This work with all its contents, does not guarantee correctness, completion, quality or correctness of the provided information. Misinformation or misprints cannot be completely eliminated.

Printed in Great Britain
by Amazon